Profiles of the Presidents

THEODORE ROOSEVELT

★ ★ ★

Profiles of the Presidents

THEODORE ROOSEVELT

by Robert Green

GULF GATE LIBRARY
7112 CURTISS AVENUE
SARASOTA, FL 34231

Content Adviser: John Allen Gable, Ph.D., Executive Director, The Theodore Roosevelt Association, Oyster Bay, New York
Reading Adviser: Dr. Linda D. Labbo, Department of Reading Education, College of Education, The University of Georgia

COMPASS POINT BOOKS ✦ MINNEAPOLIS, MINNESOTA

Compass Point Books
3109 West 50th Street, #115
Minneapolis, MN 55410

Visit Compass Point Books on the Internet at *www.compasspointbooks.com*
or e-mail your request to *custserv@compasspointbooks.com*

Photographs ©: Hulton/Archive by Getty Images, cover, 3, 7, 11 (bottom), 15, 16, 20, 22, 24, 27, 29, 32, 34, 37, 39, 42, 43, 44, 46, 48, 49, 54 (right), 55 (right), 56 (right, all), 57, 58 (all), 59 (right); Corbis, 8, 14, 19 (top), 28, 36; Theodore Roosevelt Collection, Harvard College Library, 9 (all), 10, 11 (top), 19 (bottom), 21, 38, 54 (left), 55 (left); North Wind Picture Archives, 12, 23, 25, 30, 35; Bettmann/Corbis, 13, 18, 45, 47 (top), 59 (top left); N. Carter/North Wind Picture Archives, 17; Library of Congress, 26, 56 (left); White House Collection, Courtesy White House Historical Association (image #56), 31; Underwood & Underwood/Corbis, 41; Lee Snider/Corbis, 50, 59 (bottom left).

Editors: E. Russell Primm, Emily J. Dolbear, Melissa McDaniel, and Catherine Neitge
Photo Researcher: Svetlana Zhurkina
Photo Selector: Linda S. Koutris
Designer/Page Production: The Design Lab/Les Tranby
Cartographer: XNR Productions, Inc.

Library of Congress Cataloging-in-Publication Data
Green, Robert, 1969–
  Theodore Roosevelt / by Robert Green.
    p. cm.— (Profiles of the presidents)
Summary: Biography of the twenty-sixth president of the United States, discussing his personal life, education, and political career. Includes bibliographical references (p.) and index.
  ISBN 0-7565-0272-1 (hardcover)
  1. Roosevelt, Theodore, 1858–1919—Juvenile literature. 2. Presidents—United States—Biography—Juvenile literature. [1. Roosevelt, Theodore, 1858–1919. 2. Presidents.] I. Title. II. Series.
  E757 .G735 2003
  973.91'1'092—dc21   2002010048

Table of Contents

★   ★   ★

*NOTE: In this book, words that are defined in the glossary are in **bold** the first time they appear in the text.*

At the Bully Pulpit

* * *

America was a nation on the move in the early twentieth century. The Wright brothers were perfecting the motorized airplane. Henry Ford was figuring out how to build lots of automobiles quickly. In the White House, President Theodore Roosevelt was carving out a new role for the American president.

Under the **Constitution**, the president's powers are balanced by those of Congress and the Supreme Court. Theodore Roosevelt, however, often acted without checking with Congress. He believed that if he overstepped the law, the Supreme Court would let him know about it.

When Congress disagreed with his actions, Teddy Roosevelt turned to the people for support. If Roosevelt thought something was good, he called it "bully." So the White House became his "bully **pulpit**." It was a place where he could preach his vision of America's future. And preach he did—Roosevelt loved to talk.

At that time, few Americans actually heard his enthusiastic speeches. Television and radio were not yet in use. Americans, however, could read his remarks in the newspapers. Roosevelt was the first president to use the press to speak to the people. Every president since Roosevelt has followed his example.

The president is the face of the U.S. government. When Americans looked at President Theodore Roosevelt, they saw all the energy and hope of a growing country in his face. Roosevelt was determined to use the president's powers to their fullest extent. And he would have a bully time doing it.

▲ *Teddy Roosevelt delivering one of his many speeches as president*

Young Roosevelt

★ ★ ★

Theodore Roosevelt was born on October 27, 1858, in New York City. Teddy Roosevelt's father traced his family back to the rich Dutch merchants who had helped New York to become America's leading financial city. Theodore Roosevelt Sr. was a banker and an importer. He was also active in New York's Republican Party. His son would later lead this same political party.

Roosevelt's birthplace in New York ▶

Teddy Roosevelt's mother, Martha Bulloch, came from a wealthy Georgia family. She was a woman of

▲ *Teddy's parents, Theodore Roosevelt Sr. and Martha Bulloch Roosevelt*

strong opinions. Roosevelt's parents were on opposite sides during the Civil War (1861–1865). Martha supported the South; Theodore Sr. supported the North. Teddy sided with his father, who was his hero. A visitor in the Roosevelt house once overheard Teddy praying for God to "grind the Southern troops into powder."

Teddy was often ill as a child. He suffered from asthma, a disease that made it painful and difficult for him to breathe. Poor eyesight meant that he would wear glasses for the rest of his life. Teddy was also skinny and weak, but he was determined to grow stronger. He did exercises

Four-year-old Teddy ▶

and lifted weights regularly, and he took long walks in the countryside whenever he got the chance.

Teddy did not go to school. Instead, his wealthy parents hired tutors for him. His tutors taught him geography, history, math, and science. At a young age, Teddy was fascinated by the natural world—forests, grasslands, rivers, lakes, and all the creatures of the wild.

He brought animals into the house to study. He sometimes cut them open to study their insides! His house often reeked of formaldehyde, a chemical solution used to preserve dead animals. On one occasion, the family maid cleared a smelly collection of frogs out of Teddy's dresser drawers.

Into the Great Arena

★ ★ ★

At the age of seventeen, Teddy entered Harvard College in Cambridge, Massachusetts. When Teddy entered Harvard, he wanted to become a naturalist—a scientist who studies nature. During his junior year, Teddy's father died. After a lot of thinking, Teddy decided to try his hand at politics.

The year his father died was an important one for Teddy. That same year he met Alice Hathaway Lee. The two fell in love right away. They married in 1880, the year Teddy graduated from Harvard.

◄ Roosevelt (above) at about the time he met Alice Hathaway Lee (left)

The War of 1812 ▲

The Roosevelts returned to New York and set up a home with Teddy's mother. In New York, Teddy began to study law at Columbia University. He balanced his studies with service in the National Guard. On weekends, Teddy proudly rode horses in military exercises in New York's Central Park.

Serving in the National Guard suited Roosevelt well. He loved the active life. His interest in the military had also been growing. While still at Harvard, he began writing a book on the War of 1812. He loved learning about great battles and great leaders. He also admired the fighting spirit of soldiers. He believed that war was honorable. "All the great masterful races," he said, "have been fighting races."

Before Roosevelt finished law school, he decided to enter politics. He was eager to make his mark in the world. He was first elected to the New York State Assembly when he was only twenty-three years old. He would walk around the capitol wearing expensive clothes, his glasses perched on his nose. Everyone noticed him.

▲ *Theodore Roosevelt early in his political career*

Roosevelt had a high-minded view of politics. Like his father, he believed it was the duty of the rich to look after the poor and set a moral example. This view was a little old-fashioned, though, even in Roosevelt's day. It sometimes brought him into conflict with other Republicans.

Many wealthy **industrialists**, merchants, and bankers belonged to the Republican Party. These were the kind of people that Roosevelt had known all his life. Their backgrounds were much like his father's and grandfather's.

Roosevelt (front row, sixth from the left) with members of the Republican Notification Committee and guests

Surprisingly, Roosevelt often found himself at odds with them. He did not believe that the rich should be able to use their wealth to dominate the nation. His views startled his fellow Republicans. Roosevelt once accused a banker of being a "part of that most dangerous of all dangerous classes, the wealthy criminal class."

Some Republicans distrusted Roosevelt because of his criticism of the rich. They admitted, however, that he was making a good start in politics. Republican leaders noticed him—and so did the New York press. Reporters found Roosevelt lively and interesting. They thought he brought some color to the dull political world.

Out West and Back East

★ ★ ★

Roosevelt's life as a politician was soon interrupted. In February 1884, his daughter Alice was born. Two days later, Roosevelt's wife died. On the same day, his mother died of typhoid fever.

Roosevelt loved public life, but he loved his family much more. His family was the anchor that gave him the strength to go out and do battle in the political arena. Losing two very important people left Roosevelt unsure of himself. He decided to quit politics.

◀ Roosevelt's oldest daughter, Alice

Roosevelt in the ▶
Dakota Badlands
shortly after his
wife's death

He left baby Alice with his sister and headed west to
Dakota Territory. In those days, the Dakotas were still
wild and empty. Roosevelt bought a herd of cattle. He
threw himself into the life of a cowboy. He learned how
to run a ranch and get along with the other ranchers.
Slowly, the wealthy New Yorker won the trust of the other
men in Dakota Territory.

Roosevelt loved the West. It was a wild place of great beauty. It was also a land where people had to struggle to survive. He felt that the greatness of the American landscape and the greatness of the American people came together in the West.

While living in Dakota Territory, Roosevelt wrote about his adventures in the West. Reviewers praised the work. It proved Roosevelt's skill as a writer. Roosevelt already knew that he gave good political speeches. Now he had learned that he could put his deepest thoughts and feelings into printed words that touched people.

◀ *Roosevelt's cabin in North Dakota*

Roosevelt was a ▲
respected writer.

Even if Roosevelt had never become president, he would have been well known for his writing. During his lifetime, he wrote twenty-four books and many magazine articles. It seemed he had something to say about almost every subject.

While still in Dakota Territory, Roosevelt remembered a childhood friend named Edith Kermit Carow. Edith was one of Roosevelt's earliest female friends, and he never quite forgot about her. The two decided to marry.

The wedding took place in London, England. Once again, Roosevelt would have the family life that he missed so much. After a time, Teddy and Edith had four sons and a daughter together. Edith also proved to be the most faithful supporter in his political life.

After two years as a rancher, Roosevelt longed to get back into politics. He took a job with the U.S. Civil Service Commission in Washington, D.C. This group oversaw the hiring of government em-

◄ *Edith Kermit Carow Roosevelt (above) and the Roosevelt children in 1895 with their parents. Another son, Quentin, was born in 1897.*

ployees. This may not have seemed like an important job, but Roosevelt threw himself into it anyway. Roosevelt was a very ambitious man.

William Strong ▲
believed Roosevelt
could help him rid
New York City of
political corruption.

Roosevelt worked hard to get fairer hiring practices in government. He wanted to make sure that people were hired for their skills and not for their connections. He also tried to uncover **corruption**. Roosevelt was willing to "let the chips fall where they may." Both Republicans and Democrats were caught in the scandals that followed.

Roosevelt's attack on corrupt politicians caught the attention of New York City mayor William L. Strong. Strong himself was in a fight to rid New York politics of corruption. He appointed Roosevelt to the New York City Board of Police Commissioners, which voted him president.

Roosevelt reported for work at police headquarters in downtown Manhattan in 1895. He found a police force riddled with corruption. Gambling dens and other illegal businesses often gave police officers money so that the police would not bother them.

The new police commissioner wanted to stamp out all of this. He threw himself into the job with his typical energy. He also brought a great deal of flair to his new job. He wore the blue uniform of a New York City police officer, but he added a sash and a pink shirt! He carried a patrolman's nightstick and a loaded pistol.

Roosevelt patrolled the streets at night to catch policemen sleeping on the job. The sight of the police commissioner with his glasses and his big teeth sparked the imaginations of local artists. They drew his picture for newspapers and magazines.

▼ *Roosevelt as president of the New York City Board of Police Commissioners*

Roosevelt soon became a popular figure. People admired his honesty and loved his comical outfit. His fame spread around the country and even beyond the United States. In London, his adventures as police commissioner were written about in the *London Times*.

A political cartoon of New York Police Commissioner Theodore Roosevelt and Mayor William Strong (driving the cart)

Even though Roosevelt was popular with the newspapers, many officials disliked him. Roosevelt felt like a bear that had disturbed a beehive while trying to get some honey. He was stung from all directions. Local politicians wanted to get rid of him. So did policemen who got rich from corruption. Even other police commissioners resented all the attention he got.

"The Great Day of My Life"

★   ★   ★

▲ As assistant secretary of the navy, Roosevelt was eager for a war.

President William Mc-Kinley rescued Roosevelt by naming him assistant secretary of the navy in 1897. Roosevelt had long believed that America needed a strong navy if it wanted to play a big role in the world. Ever since he was a child, he had loved ships and naval history. Now, as second in command of the U.S. Navy, Roosevelt tried to increase its size. He also tried to find a war in which to use it. "This country needs a war," he declared.

Cuban rebels ▲ Roosevelt believed that European powers had no right to get involved in the Western Hemisphere. He believed that the United States should be the only great power in the region. A **rebellion** had broken out on the island of Cuba in the Caribbean Sea. Cuba had long been controlled by Spain. Roosevelt wanted to support the rebels and throw out the Spanish.

On February 15, 1898, the *Maine*, an American warship, sank off the shores of Cuba. More than two hundred American sailors died. This convinced the U.S. government to enter the war. Now that Roosevelt had his war, he quit his job as assistant secretary of the navy. "I don't want to be in the office during the war," he said. "I want to be at the front."

▾ *The* Maine *just before its fatal voyage to Cuba*

Roosevelt (center) ▶
led the Rough Riders.

Roosevelt organized a **cavalry** unit known as the Rough Riders. Some Rough Riders were rough-and-tumble cowboys from the West. Others were horsemen from East Coast universities. They were not professional soldiers, but they could all ride horses and handle rifles. They also were all willing to follow Lieutenant Colonel Theodore Roosevelt into battle.

Roosevelt was the spirit of the Rough Riders, and that spirit was recklessness. He longed to lead a battle charge. His chance came when the army needed the Rough Riders to take the hills in front of the Cuban city of Santiago. Roosevelt led his men on charges up two hills through enemy fire. "San Juan was the great day of my life," he later wrote.

The Spanish-American War soon ended, and Roosevelt was the war's biggest hero. He and his Rough Riders played only a small role in the war, but the public loved them.

▲ *Roosevelt during his command of the Rough Riders*

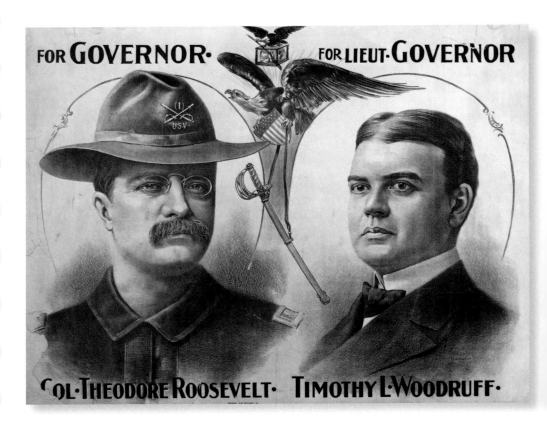

FOR GOVERNOR·   **FOR LIEUT· GOVERNOR**

·COL·THEODORE ROOSEVELT·   TIMOTHY L·WOODRUFF·

A campaign poster ▲ for the 1898 New York election with Roosevelt and running mate Timothy Woodruff

The Rough Riders' fame gave Roosevelt the chance to get back into politics. The Republican Party of New York needed someone to run for governor in 1898. Roosevelt's wartime heroics helped him win that election.

As governor, Roosevelt raised taxes on the largest and most powerful businesses in the state. This angered his old enemies in big business and in the Republican Party. Roosevelt also threatened the jobs of Republican politicians by making sure that people were promoted based on

◄ *This political cartoon from 1899 made fun of Roosevelt's sometimes tense relationship with Republican politicians.*

how well they did their job. Government employees were forced to perform well or risk losing their jobs.

Almost as soon as Roosevelt became governor, Republican Party leaders wanted to get rid of him. He was too famous to ignore, but too much trouble to keep as governor. Senator Thomas Platt, the head of New York's Republican Party, came up with a way to solve this problem. He urged Roosevelt to run for vice president under President William McKinley in 1900.

When McKinley was elected president, New York Republicans were free of Roosevelt's meddling. The national Republican leadership was not so happy, though. Roosevelt was now their problem. "Don't any of you realize," Republican leader Mark Hanna asked, "that there is only one life between this madman and the White House?"

On September 6, 1901, a man named Leon Czolgosz shot President McKinley in Buffalo, New York. McKinley died on September 14, 1901. That same day, Roosevelt was sworn in as the twenty-sixth president of the United States. Only forty-two years old, he became the youngest president in American history. "Now look," Hanna swore, "that damned cowboy is president of the United States!"

Leon Czolgosz ▼

A Bully Job

★ ★ ★

Roosevelt wanted
Americans to have
confidence in his abili-
ty to take over as pres-
ident. He promised to
continue McKinley's
policies. This proved
to be a tall order for
Roosevelt. He was
nothing if not his own
man. He could not
keep his opinions to
himself, even when he
tried. "His personali-
ty," remarked a friend, "so crowds the room that the
walls are worn thin and threaten to burst outward."

▲ *A portrait of
President Roosevelt
from the White
House collection.
It was painted
by John Singer
Sargent.*

Roosevelt tried to reshape the presidency in his own
image. In doing so, he ran up against some of the most

powerful people and businesses in the United States. When Roosevelt entered the White House, business had almost unlimited power in the United States. Large companies were able to squash their smaller competition. Roosevelt wanted to limit the power of these large businesses, known as **trusts.**

Roosevelt first set his sights on the Northern Securities Company. This company was owned by J. Pierpont Morgan, one of the richest men in the country. Morgan's company controlled railroads, and it fixed prices to keep other companies from competing.

Roosevelt attacked ▼ the monopoly on railroads.

Roosevelt tried to keep Morgan from setting unfair prices. Then the Supreme Court ruled that Morgan's company was a monopoly—a business that controls an entire industry and keeps out competition. After this, Morgan's company was broken up. The newspapers called the new president a "trustbuster."

To fight the trusts,

Roosevelt pushed through the Hepburn Act of 1906. This act gave the government the power to **regulate** the rates for goods shipped by train. Companies could now send their goods from state to state at the same rate. This blocked the shippers from giving some people better rates than others.

Roosevelt also pushed through the Pure Food and Drug Act. With this law, the government could make sure that food and medicines were safe. It has been important ever since in protecting the American people.

Roosevelt also wanted to ensure that products were stored and shipped safely. To do this, he gave the Department of Agriculture the power to inspect warehouses and stockyards.

Government regulation of business is normal today, but it wasn't during Roosevelt's time. Roosevelt was accused of interfering with business. He just ignored those complaints. "My business," he said, "is to see fair play among all men, **capitalists** or wage workers."

Roosevelt did much for workers. He helped create safety standards in the workplace. He also supported shortening the working day and saw that fairer tax laws were passed.

Roosevelt improved ▼
conditions for
workers like those at
this California fruit
packing plant.

Roosevelt didn't support everything workers did, however. In 1902, the United Mine Workers began a national **strike.** Roosevelt feared the country would face a coal shortage. He stepped in to personally solve the dispute between workers and mine owners. He prepared the National Guard to take over running the mines and keep the peace if violence broke out. Roosevelt was taking on powers far beyond those of earlier presidents.

▾ *Miners threatened to strike in 1902.*

Roosevelt believed it ▶
was important to
preserve America's
forests and other
natural resources.

Roosevelt also used his power as president to try to preserve America's beautiful land and many natural resources. As president, he used the bully pulpit to convince members of Congress to set aside America's natural resources for the future. Roosevelt warned politicians and the American public that forests, water, and soil were not unlimited. He reminded people that it was important to conserve these resources so they would be able to hand down an equally beautiful and abundant country to their children.

In 1902, he supported the Newlands Reclamation Act. This created water projects all over the country, including the Roosevelt Dam in Arizona. In addition, he defeated plans to develop the Muscle Shoals area of the Tennessee River. Roosevelt was pitting himself against private business once again. This time, however, he had the support of politicians from both political parties.

▲ *The Roosevelt Dam in Arizona was built as part of Roosevelt's Newlands Reclamation Act.*

Roosevelt worked ▶
for many years to
preserve
Yellowstone
National Park. He
came to inspect the
park in 1903.

Roosevelt had seen much beautiful land in his treks across the American West. But he had also seen the effects of industry on the landscape. Mining, factories, logging, and other businesses had laid waste to once-clean rivers and forests. During Roosevelt's presidency, he helped protect more than 230 million acres (93 million hectares) of land.

Roosevelt organized the Forest Service to watch over the new national forests that were being created. He named his friend Gifford Pinchot to lead the Forest Service. Pinchot shared Roosevelt's passion for the American wilderness. Working with Pinchot, Roosevelt did a better job of protecting the environment than almost any other president has.

▲ *Gifford Pinchot*

The Bull Moose

★ ★ ★

In 1904, Theodore Roosevelt was elected to a full term as president. He was very popular, so it was an easy win.

Life in the White House seemed to suit Roosevelt. "I like being president," he once stated. The White House was filled with activity when Roosevelt lived there. Rough Riders came to visit. Famous boxers were invited to spar with the president.

Roosevelt's eldest daughter, Alice, was an adult by this time, but his five youngest children had the run of the White House. President Roosevelt could often be found having pillow fights or playing cowboys and Indians with his children. "You must always remember that the president is about six," remarked a British official.

Being elected president rather than taking over for a president gave Roosevelt more confidence. He tried to make the United States one of the world's great powers.

◀ *Roosevelt's 1905 inauguration speech*

Elihu Root ▲

His **cabinet** included Elihu Root, who served as secretary of war and later as secretary of state. The president sometimes acted like a bull in a china shop, but Root was always careful about what he said. He helped Roosevelt greatly.

One of Roosevelt's greatest victories in expanding American power was the building of the Panama Canal. Roosevelt had long dreamed of a way to shorten the sea route between the eastern and western United States.

In 1902, Congress finally approved carving a canal through the narrow region of Panama in Central America. At that time, Panama belonged to the country of Colombia. The Colombians refused to accept the canal plan. Rebels in Panama, encouraged by Roosevelt, rose up in 1903 and declared Panama's independence. Roosevelt sent the U.S. Navy to Panama to keep the Colombians at bay. Panama became an independent country.

Roosevelt was delighted. "I took Panama," he once remarked. The new government of Panama leased a 10-mile (16-km)-wide zone for the construction of the canal. American troops would protect the canal, but ships of all countries could pass through it. In 1906, Roosevelt sailed to Panama to inspect the digging of the canal. He was the first U.S. president to leave the United States while in office.

▼ *Construction of the Panama Canal*

Roosevelt (center) led peace talks between Russian and Japanese leaders in 1905.

Roosevelt's policies made the United States important on the international stage. When Japan and Russia went to war, for example, Roosevelt worked out a peace settlement. For his efforts, he won the 1906 Nobel Peace Prize.

Some Americans, such as the writer Mark Twain, believed that Roosevelt wanted the United States to be an **empire**. They disliked Roosevelt's plans to expand America's power beyond the United States. To this Roosevelt simply replied: "I fail to understand how any man can be anything but an **expansionist**."

Roosevelt's beliefs can be seen in one of his favorite sayings: "Speak softly and carry a big stick." The greatest display of Roosevelt's big-stick attitude came in 1907

when he sent the U.S. Navy on a goodwill tour of the world. It was meant to show the power of the United States, but many people thought it was more likely to arouse anger than goodwill.

▲ *American battleships on Roosevelt's goodwill tour*

Roosevelt (left) ▶
with William
Howard Taft

When Roosevelt was elected in 1904, he promised not to run for another term as president. So, as Roosevelt's term came to a close, he paved the way for his secretary of war, William Howard Taft, to replace him as president. On March 4, 1909, Teddy Roosevelt left the White House.

Roosevelt worked for Taft's election because he believed that Taft would continue his policies. Taft won the election.

★

◄ A certificate
promoting the
1912 presidential
campaign of
Roosevelt and
running mate
Hiram Johnson

Roosevelt soon noticed that Taft had a mind of his own. So Roosevelt jumped back into politics. "My hat is in the ring," he declared. Roosevelt left the Republican Party and joined the Progressive Party. When Taft ran for reelection in 1912, Roosevelt declared himself "as fit as a bull moose" for the fight against Taft. Reporters took to calling Roosevelt's new party the Bull Moose Party.

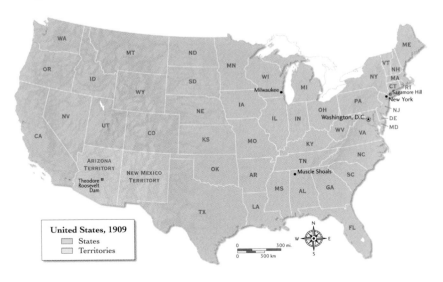

The Bull Moose needed all his strength, as it happened. In Milwaukee, Wisconsin, during the 1912 campaign, someone fired a bullet into Roosevelt's chest. The slug was slowed by an eyeglass case and his folded speech. The old Rough Rider continued his speech.

Woodrow Wilson ▼

When the election came around, a lot of Republicans voted for Roosevelt. He actually got more votes than Taft. This split among Republicans opened the way for Democrat Woodrow Wilson to win the election. Roosevelt still stands as the only third-party **candidate** to beat a Republican or Democrat in a national election.

As a private citizen once more, Roosevelt was a bundle of energy. He went hunting in Africa and explored part of the Amazon River in South America. He remained a popular figure in the United States. A story of him refusing to shoot an injured bear on a hunting trip led a toy maker to name the teddy bear after Roosevelt. When Roosevelt visited Oxford University in England, students placed a toy bear in his path and lowered one from the ceiling.

▼ *Roosevelt during his 1909 hunting trip in Africa*

Roosevelt's fame kept him in the public eye. When World War I (1914–1918) began in Europe, Roosevelt argued that the United States should become involved. The United States finally entered the war in 1917. In 1918, the final year of the war, Roosevelt got news that his son Quentin's plane had been shot down by the Germans. His son was dead. Roosevelt himself had started the airborne section of the American military. His son was one of the first American airmen killed. It is said Roosevelt never recovered from the death of his youngest child.

By the end of the war, Republicans had forgiven Roosevelt for having started the Bull Moose Party. They hoped Roosevelt would run for president in 1920. But he did not get the chance. His health had been failing, and he died on January 6, 1919. He was sixty-one. Roosevelt was buried in Oyster Bay Cove, New York, near the site of his sprawling home on Sagamore Hill.

The gravestone of Theodore and Edith Roosevelt. Mrs. Roosevelt died in 1948. She was eighty-seven.

Reporters wrote long articles honoring the former president. Roosevelt had created the White House pressroom to deal with reporters. They in turn made him the first celebrity president. Roosevelt had made the presidency the center of political life. He also made the presidency a little more like Teddy Roosevelt.

GLOSSARY

★ ★ ★

cabinet—a president's group of advisers who are the heads of government departments

candidate—someone running for office in an election

capitalists—wealthy people who often own businesses

cavalry—an army unit on horseback

Constitution—the document stating the basic laws of the United States

corruption—willingness to do things that are wrong or illegal

empire—a country that controls areas far beyond its borders

expansionist—someone who thinks a country should become larger

industrialists—people who own factories

pulpit—a platform where a preacher speaks

rebellion—an armed uprising against the government

regulate—to make rules that businesses must follow

strike—when people refuse to work, hoping to force their company to agree to their demands

trusts—businesses so large that other companies can't compete

THEODORE ROOSEVELT'S LIFE AT A GLANCE

★ ★ ★

PERSONAL

Nicknames:	TR, Trustbuster, Teddy
Birthdate:	October 27, 1858
Birthplace:	New York City, New York
Father's name:	Theodore Roosevelt
Mother's name:	Martha Bulloch Roosevelt
Education:	Graduated from Harvard College in 1880
Wives' names:	Alice Hathaway Lee Roosevelt (1861–1884); Edith Kermit Carow Roosevelt (1861–1948)
Married:	October 27, 1880; December 2, 1886
Children:	Alice Lee Roosevelt (1884–1980); Theodore Roosevelt (1887–1944); Kermit Roosevelt (1889–1943); Ethel Carow Roosevelt (1891–1977); Archibald Bulloch Roosevelt (1894–1979); Quentin Roosevelt (1897–1918)
Died:	January 6, 1919, in Oyster Bay Cove, New York
Buried:	Youngs Memorial Cemetery in Oyster Bay, New York

PUBLIC

Occupation before presidency: Author, public official

Occupation after presidency: Writer

Military service: Colonel of the Rough Riders in the Spanish-American War

Other government positions: State assemblyman; civil service commissioner; president of the board of police commissioners in New York City; assistant secretary of the navy; governor of New York; vice president

Political party: Republican

Vice president: Charles Warren Fairbanks (1905–1909)

Dates in office: September 14, 1901–March 4, 1909

Presidential opponents: Alton B. Parker (Democrat), 1904; William Howard Taft (Republican), Woodrow Wilson (Democrat), 1912

Number of votes (Electoral College): 7,628,461 of 12,712,684 (336 of 476), 1904; 4,118,571 of 13,901,838 (88 of 531), 1912

Selected Writings: *The Naval War of 1812* (1882), *The Winning of the West* (1889–1896), *The Rough Riders* (1899), *African Game Trails* (1910), *America and the World War* (1915)

Theodore Roosevelt's Cabinet

Secretary of state:
John M. Hay (1901–1905)
Elihu Root (1905–1909)
Robert Bacon (1909)

Secretary of the treasury:
Lyman J. Gage (1901–1902)
Leslie M. Shaw (1902–1907)
George B. Cortelyou (1907–1909)

Secretary of war:
Elihu Root (1901–1904)
William H. Taft (1904–1908)
Luke E. Wright (1908–1909)

Attorney general:
Philander C. Knox (1901–1904)
William H. Moody (1904–1906)
Charles J. Bonaparte (1906–1909)

Postmaster general:
Charles Emory Smith (1901–1902)
Henry C. Payne (1902–1904)
Robert J. Wynne (1904–1905)
George B. Cortelyou (1905–1907)
George von L. Meyer (1907–1909)

Secretary of the navy:
James D. Long (1901–1902)
William H. Moody (1902–1904)
Paul Morton (1904–1905)
Charles J. Bonaparte (1905–1906)
Victor H. Metcalf (1906–1908)
Truman H. Newberry (1908–1909)

Secretary of the interior:
Ethan A. Hitchcock (1901–1907)
James R. Garfield (1907–1909)

Secretary of agriculture:
James Wilson (1901–1909)

Secretary of commerce and labor:
George B. Cortelyou (1903–1904)
Victor H. Metcalf (1904–1906)
Oscar S. Straus (1906–1909)

THEODORE ROOSEVELT'S LIFE AND TIMES

★ ★ ★

ROOSEVELT'S LIFE		WORLD EVENTS

October 27, Roosevelt is born in New York City	1858	1858 — English scientist Charles Darwin (above) presents his theory of evolution
	1860	1860 — Austrian composer Gustav Mahler is born in Kalischt (now in Austria)
		1865 — *Tristan and Isolde,* by German composer Richard Wagner, opens in Munich

ROOSEVELT'S LIFE		WORLD EVENTS	
		1868	Louisa May Alcott publishes *Little Women*
	1870		The transcontinental railroad across the United States is completed
Enters Harvard College	1876	1876	Alexander Graham Bell uses the first telephone to speak to his assistant, Thomas Watson
		1877	German inventor Nikolaus A. Otto works on what will become the internal combustion engine for automobiles
		1879	Electric lights are invented
Graduates from Harvard College; marries Alice Hathaway Lee	1880 **1880**		
Elected to the New York State Assembly	1881	1882	Thomas Edison builds a power station
February 14, both his wife and his mother die; after finishing term, Roosevelt retreats to Dakota Territory	1884	1884	Mark Twain (right) publishes *The Adventures of Huckleberry Finn*

ROOSEVELT'S LIFE

Returns to New York to run for mayor; is defeated; marries Edith Kermit Carow	1886
Serves on the United States Civil Service Commission	1889– 1895
Becomes president of the New York City Board of Police Commissioners	1895
Named assistant secretary of the navy; leads his Rough Riders (below) up San Juan Hill in Cuba during the Spanish-American War	1898

1890

WORLD EVENTS

1886	Grover Cleveland dedicates the Statue of Liberty in New York
	Bombing in Haymarket Square, Chicago (below), due to labor unrest

1893	Women gain voting privileges in New Zealand, the first country to take such a step
1896	The Olympic Games are held for the first time in recent history, in Athens, Greece (below)

ROOSEVELT'S LIFE		WORLD EVENTS
Elected governor of New York	1898	
	1899	Isadora Duncan (below), one of the founders of modern dance, makes her debut in Chicago
Elected vice president under William McKinley	1900	

1900

	1901	Queen Victoria dies in England at age eighty-one
Becomes the twenty-sixth president when McKinley is assassinated in September	1901	

★

ROOSEVELT'S LIFE

1902

The government sues Northern Securities Company under the Sherman Anti-Trust Act

The United Mine Workers go on strike; Roosevelt personally tries to work out a deal between the workers and the owners

Signs a treaty with Panama to build a canal (below)

Presidential Election Results:	Popular Votes	Electoral Votes
1904 Theodore Roosevelt	7,628,461	336
Alton B. Parker	5,084,223	140

1905

Starts the United States Forest Service

Helps negotiate the end of the Russo-Japanese War

1906

Wins the Nobel Peace Prize

WORLD EVENTS

1903 Brothers Orville and Wilbur Wright successfully fly a powered airplane (below)

1904 The Russo–Japanese War begins

1905

1906 Earthquake and fire destroy San Francisco, killing hundreds (above)

ROOSEVELT'S LIFE

Congress passes the   1907
Meat Inspection Act
and the Pure Food and
Drug Act

Sends the U.S. Navy   1908
on a tour of the
world, displaying
America's power

Runs for president   1912
as a member of the
Progressive Party
(above); gets more
votes than Republican
president William
Howard Taft but loses
to Democrat
Woodrow Wilson

Maps the Rio da   1914
Divuda, a river in
Brazil that is later
renamed Rio Roosevelt
in his honor

January 6, dies at his   1919
home in Oyster Bay
Cove, New York

WORLD EVENTS

1907   German-born
physicist Albert
Einstein develops his
equation for energy,
$E=MC^2$

1909   The National
Association for the
Advancement of
Colored People
(NAACP) is founded

1913   Henry Ford begins to
use standard assembly
lines to produce
automobiles (above)

1914   Archduke Francis
Ferdinand is
assassinated,
launching World
War I

1916   Einstein publishes his
general theory of
relativity

1919   World War I peace
conference begins at
Versailles, France

1910

UNDERSTANDING THEODORE ROOSEVELT AND HIS PRESIDENCY

★　★　★

IN THE LIBRARY

Armstrong, Jennifer. *Theodore Roosevelt: Letters from a Young Coal Miner.* Delray Beach, Fla.: Winslow Press, 2001.

Fritz, Jean. *Bully for You, Teddy Roosevelt!.* New York: Putnam, 1991.

Harness, Cheryl. *Young Teddy Roosevelt.* Washington, D.C.: National Geographic Society, 1998.

Kozar, Richard. *Theodore Roosevelt and the Exploration of the Amazon Basin.* Broomall, Pa.: Chelsea House, 2000.

Meltzer, Milton. *Theodore Roosevelt and His America.* New York: Franklin Watts, 1994.

Parks, Edd Winfield. *Teddy Roosevelt: Young Rough Rider.* New York: Simon & Schuster, 1989.

Sateren, Shelley Swanson, ed. *Boyhood Diary of Theodore Roosevelt 1869–1870.* Mankato, Minn.: Blue Earth Books/Capstone Press, 2001.

Whitelaw, Nancy. *Theodore Roosevelt Takes Charge.* Morton Grove, Ill.: Albert Whitman & Company, 1992.

ON THE WEB

About Theodore Roosevelt
http://www.theodoreroosevelt.org/
For a biography, pictures, quotes, and more

Almanac of the Theodore Roosevelt/Amazon Expedition
http://www.theodore-roosevelt.com/trbrazil.html
For pictures from Roosevelt's trip to Brazil

Theodore Roosevelt: His Life and Times on Film
http://memory.loc.gov/ammem/trfhtml/
To look through film and sound recordings of Roosevelt

The White House—Theodore Roosevelt
http://www.whitehouse.gov/history/presidents/tr26.html
For a brief life story

ROOSEVELT HISTORIC SITES ACROSS THE COUNTRY

**Theodore Roosevelt
Birthplace National Historic Site**
28 East 20th Street
New York, NY 10003
212/260-1616
To visit the spot where Roosevelt
lived until he was fourteen

**Theodore Roosevelt
National Park**
P.O. Box 7
Medora, ND 58645
701/623-4466
To visit Roosevelt's cabin
in the Badlands

Sagamore Hill
20 Sagamore Hill Road
Oyster Bay, NY 11771
516/922-4447
To tour Roosevelt's home and
visit a museum devoted to his life

Mount Rushmore
P.O. Box 268
Keystone, SD 57751
603/574-2523
To see a giant sculpture of
Roosevelt as well as Presidents
Washington, Jefferson, and Lincoln

THE U.S. PRESIDENTS
(Years in Office)

★ ★ ★

1. **George Washington**
   (March 4, 1789-March 3, 1797)
2. **John Adams**
   (March 4, 1797-March 3, 1801)
3. **Thomas Jefferson**
   (March 4, 1801-March 3, 1809)
4. **James Madison**
   (March 4, 1809-March 3, 1817)
5. **James Monroe**
   (March 4, 1817-March 3, 1825)
6. **John Quincy Adams**
   (March 4, 1825-March 3, 1829)
7. **Andrew Jackson**
   (March 4, 1829-March 3, 1837)
8. **Martin Van Buren**
   (March 4, 1837-March 3, 1841)
9. **William Henry Harrison**
   (March 6, 1841-April 4, 1841)
10. **John Tyler**
    (April 6, 1841-March 3, 1845)
11. **James K. Polk**
    (March 4, 1845-March 3, 1849)
12. **Zachary Taylor**
    (March 5, 1849-July 9, 1850)
13. **Millard Fillmore**
    (July 10, 1850-March 3, 1853)
14. **Franklin Pierce**
    (March 4, 1853-March 3, 1857)
15. **James Buchanan**
    (March 4, 1857-March 3, 1861)
16. **Abraham Lincoln**
    (March 4, 1861-April 15, 1865)
17. **Andrew Johnson**
    (April 15, 1865-March 3, 1869)

18. **Ulysses S. Grant**
    (March 4, 1869-March 3, 1877)
19. **Rutherford B. Hayes**
    (March 4, 1877-March 3, 1881)
20. **James Garfield**
    (March 4, 1881-Sept 19, 1881)
21. **Chester Arthur**
    (Sept 20, 1881-March 3, 1885)
22. **Grover Cleveland**
    (March 4, 1885-March 3, 1889)
23. **Benjamin Harrison**
    (March 4, 1889-March 3, 1893)
24. **Grover Cleveland**
    (March 4, 1893-March 3, 1897)
25. **William McKinley**
    (March 4, 1897-
    September 14, 1901)
26. **Theodore Roosevelt**
    (September 14, 1901-
    March 3, 1909)
27. **William Howard Taft**
    (March 4, 1909-March 3, 1913)
28. **Woodrow Wilson**
    (March 4, 1913-March 3, 1921)
29. **Warren G. Harding**
    (March 4, 1921-August 2, 1923)
30. **Calvin Coolidge**
    (August 3, 1923-March 3, 1929)
31. **Herbert Hoover**
    (March 4, 1929-March 3, 1933)
32. **Franklin D. Roosevelt**
    (March 4, 1933-April 12, 1945)

33. **Harry S. Truman**
    (April 12, 1945-
    January 20, 1953)
34. **Dwight D. Eisenhower**
    (January 20, 1953-
    January 20, 1961)
35. **John F. Kennedy**
    (January 20, 1961-
    November 22, 1963)
36. **Lyndon B. Johnson**
    (November 22, 1963-
    January 20, 1969)
37. **Richard M. Nixon**
    (January 20, 1969-
    August 9, 1974)
38. **Gerald R. Ford**
    (August 9, 1974-
    January 20, 1977)
39. **James Earl Carter**
    (January 20, 1977-
    January 20, 1981)
40. **Ronald Reagan**
    (January 20, 1981-
    January 20, 1989)
41. **George H. W. Bush**
    (January 20, 1989-
    January 20, 1993)
42. **William Jefferson Clinton**
    (January 20, 1993-
    January 20, 2001)
43. **George W. Bush**
    (January 20, 2001-)

INDEX

★ ★ ★

Index

ABOUT THE AUTHOR

Robert Green holds a master's degree in journalism from New York University and a bachelor's degree in English literature from Boston University.

Green is the author of two other titles in this series—*Woodrow Wilson* and *Richard Nixon*—and of twenty other books for young readers, including *Modern Nations of the World: China* and *Modern Nations of the World: Taiwan*. He has also written biographies of such historical figures as Julius Caesar, Cleopatra, and Alexander the Great. Currently, Green lives in Taiwan and is an editor for a Taiwanese magazine.